Candle Time

Happy Birthday!

Denise M. Jordan

Heinemann Library
Chicago, Illinois

© 2002 Reed Educational & Professional Publishing
Published by Heinemann Library,
an imprint of Reed Educational & Professional Publishing,
Chicago, Illinois

Customer Service 888-454-2279
Visit our website at www.heinemannlibrary.com

All rights reserved. No part of this publication may be reproduced or transmitted in any form or by any means, electronic or mechanical, including photocopying, recording, taping, or any information storage and retrieval system, without permission in writing from the publisher.

Designed by Sue Emerson, Heinemann Library; Page layout by Ginkgo Creative, Inc.
Printed and bound in the U.S.A. by Lake Book

06 05 04 03 02
10 9 8 7 6 5 4 3 2 1

Library of Congress Cataloging-in-Publication Data
Jordan, Denise M.
   Happy birthday! / Denise Jordan.
      p. cm. — (Candle time)
Includes index.
Summary: Introduces the symbols, celebration, and traditions of birthdays.
   ISBN: 1-58810-526-1 (HC), ISBN 1-5880-735-3 (Pbk.)
   1. Birthday parties—Juvenile literature. [1. Birthdays. 2. Birthday parties.] I. Title. II. Series.
   GV1472.7.B5 J67 2002
   394.2—dc21
                              2001004630

Acknowledgments
The author and publishers are grateful to the following for permission to reproduce copyright material:
p. 4 Zave Smith/Age Foto Stock; pp. 5, 8, 11, 17, 21 Victor Englebert; p. 6 Amor Montes De Oca; pp. 9, 16, 18 TRIP/H. Rogers; pp. 10, 14, 20 Brian Seed; pp. 12, 22 Lee White/Corbis; p. 13 Craig Mitchelldyer; pp. 15, 19 David June; glossary (piñata) Gary A. Conner/DDB Stock Photo

Cover photograph courtesy of Craig Mitchelldyer

Every effort has been made to contact copyright holders of any material reproduced in this book. Any omissions will be rectified in subsequent printings if notice is given to the publisher.

Special thanks to our advisory panel for their help in the preparation of this book:

Eileen Day, Preschool Teacher
Chicago, IL

Paula Fischer, K–1 Teacher
Indianapolis, IN

Sandra Gilbert,
Library Media Specialist
Houston, TX

Angela Leeper,
Educational Consultant
North Carolina Department
of Public Instruction
Raleigh, NC

Pam McDonald, Reading Teacher
Winter Springs, FL

Melinda Murphy,
Library Media Specialist
Houston, TX

Helen Rosenberg, MLS
Chicago, IL

Anna Marie Varakin,
Reading Instructor
Western Maryland College

Some words are shown in bold, **like this.**
You can find them in the picture glossary on page 23.

Contents

What Is a Birthday? 4
When Do People Celebrate
     Their Birthdays? 6
What Do People Do on Their Birthdays? . . 8
What Lights Are There for a Birthday? . . 10
What Do Birthday Decorations
     Look Like? 12
What Foods Do People Eat
     for a Birthday? 14
How Do Children Dress for a Birthday? . 16
What Games Do Children Play
     for a Birthday? 18
Are There Gifts for a Birthday? 20
Quiz 22
Picture Glossary 23
Note to Parents and Teachers 24
Answers to Quiz 24
Index 24

What Is a Birthday?

A birthday is a candle time.

Your birthday is the day you were born.

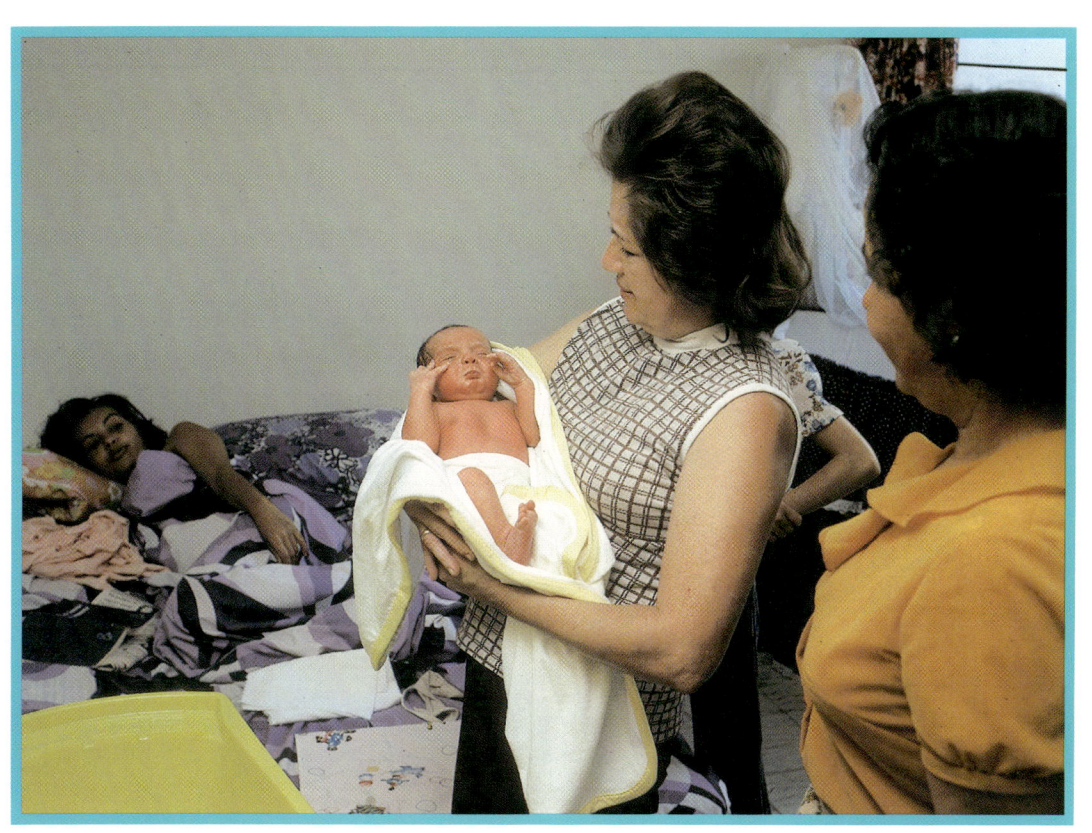

Some people are born in a hospital.

Some people are born at home.

When Do People Celebrate Their Birthdays?

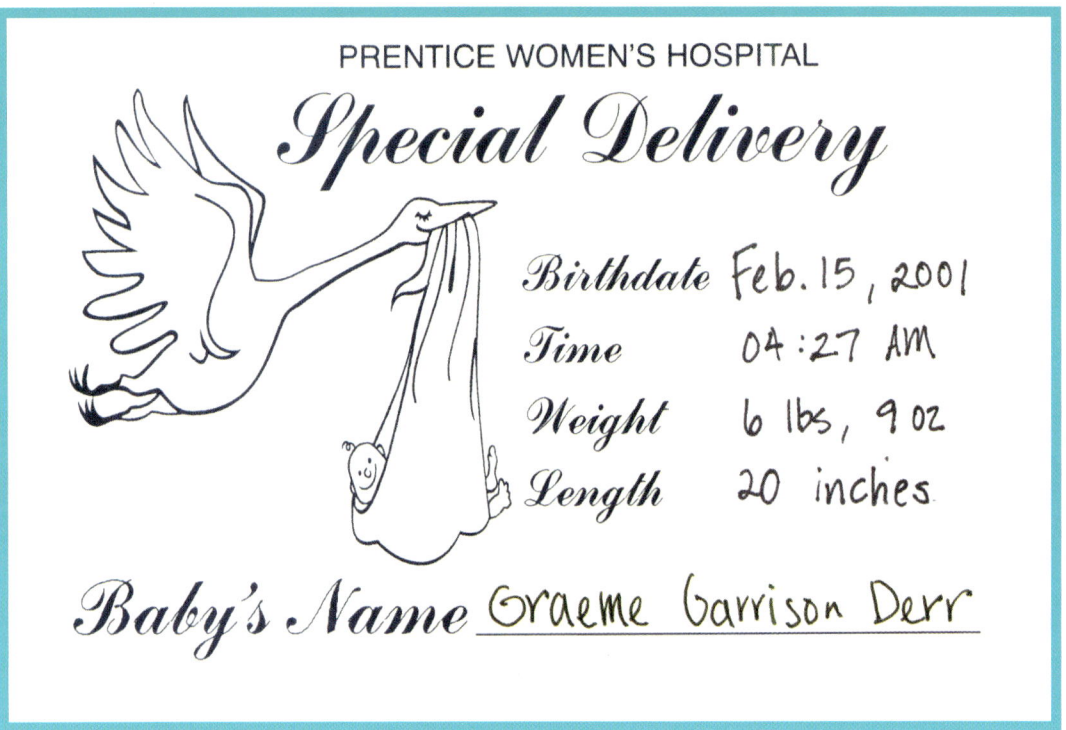

A **birth announcement** shows the day a person was born.

Every year, they celebrate their birthday on that same day.

What Do People Do on Their Birthdays?

Some people celebrate their birthdays with family and friends.

Some people have a party.

Some people go to a special place.

Most people do something fun.

What Lights Are There for a Birthday?

People light candles to celebrate their birthdays.

They put the candles on a cake.

The number of candles shows the person's age.

Some people make a wish before they blow out the candles.

What Do Birthday Decorations Look Like?

streamers

Some people decorate with balloons and **streamers**.

People can buy birthday decorations in stores.

Some families make their own decorations.

They put up signs that say Happy Birthday.

What Foods Do People Eat for a Birthday?

Some people eat their favorite food on their birthdays.

It might be hot dogs, tacos, or pizza.

Some people have cake and ice cream.

How Do Children Dress for a Birthday?

Some children get new clothes for their birthdays.

They might wear a suit or a party dress.

Others wear a T-shirt and jeans.

Some children wear party hats.

What Games Do Children Play for a Birthday?

Some children play "Pin the Tail on the Donkey."

Some children hit a **piñata**.

Candy and toys fall out when the piñata breaks.

Are There Gifts for a Birthday?

People get cards and gifts on their birthdays.

Gifts may come in the mail.

Friends may bring gifts to a birthday party.

Your birthday is a special day!

Quiz

You might see these things on a birthday.

Can you name them?

Look for the answers on page 24.

? ? ?

Picture Glossary

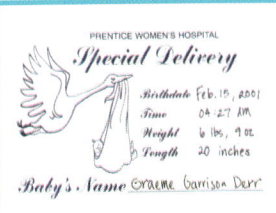
birth announcement
page 6

piñata
(peen-YAH-ta)
page 19

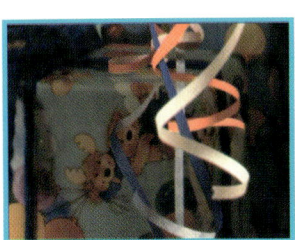
streamers
page 12

Note to Parents and Teachers

Reading for information is an important part of a child's literacy development. Learning begins with a question about something. Help children think of themselves as investigators and researchers by encouraging their questions about the world around them. Each chapter in this book begins with a question. Read the question together. Look at the pictures. Talk about what you think the answer might be. Then read the text to find out if your predictions were correct. Think of other questions you could ask about the topic, and discuss where you might find the answers. Assist children in using the picture glossary and the index to practice new vocabulary and research skills.

Index

birth announcement 6
cake 10, 15
candles 4, 10–11
cards 20

games 18–19
gifts 20–21
hot dogs 14
ice cream 15
party hats 17
"Pin the Tail on
  the Donkey" 18
piñata 19
pizza 14
streamers 12
tacos 14

Answers to quiz on page 22

balloon | sign | streamers